THESE ARE ANIMALS

Daniel Egnéus

BLOOMSBURY

LONDON OXFORD NEW YORK NEW DELHI SYDNEY

TRUMP

THESE ARE ANIMALS

Some are **wide** and some are **TALL**,
long and **thin**, round and **small**.
Prickly, squeaky, **growly**, spiny,
fierce, **loud**, sleek and shiny.

These are animals.
Come and meet them **all!**

SNAP

THESE ARE WOODLAND ANIMALS

Rabbits SQUEAK

Hedgehogs snuffle

Raccoons **CLIMB**

And woodpeckers **tap tap TAP.**

Moose **chomp** on leaves
Squirrels **nibble** on nuts

And foxes JUMP.

Deer **PRANCE** and bears
GROWWWL.

THESE ARE POLAR ANIMALS

Whales SPLASH

Seals bark – ARF ARF ARF

Polar bears have

HUGE

paws

And penguins **sliiiide.**

THESE ARE GRASSLAND ANIMALS

Giraffes have looong necks

Elephants play TRUMPET trunks

Zebras show off zig zag stripes

dungi